# 50 The Art of Salad Recipes for Home

By: Kelly Johnson

# Table of Contents

- Classic Caesar Salad
- Mediterranean Quinoa Salad
- Spinach and Strawberry Salad
- Greek Salad with Feta
- Caprese Salad with Balsamic Glaze
- Cobb Salad with Avocado
- Roasted Beet and Goat Cheese Salad
- Asian Sesame Chicken Salad
- Chickpea and Avocado Salad
- Watermelon and Feta Salad
- Arugula and Pear Salad
- Southwest Black Bean Salad
- Thai Mango Salad
- Kale and Apple Salad
- Panzanella (Bread Salad)
- Farro and Roasted Vegetable Salad
- Zucchini Noodle Salad
- Lentil Salad with Herbs
- Grilled Vegetable Salad
- Tuna Niçoise Salad
- Cabbage and Carrot Slaw
- Shrimp and Avocado Salad
- Berry Spinach Salad
- Citrus and Pomegranate Salad
- Thai Peanut Salad
- Roasted Carrot and Quinoa Salad
- Cobb Pasta Salad
- Apple and Walnut Salad
- BBQ Chicken Salad
- Caprese Pasta Salad
- Couscous and Chickpea Salad
- Taco Salad with Lime Dressing
- Mediterranean Pasta Salad
- Radish and Cucumber Salad
- Beet and Citrus Salad
- Honey Mustard Chicken Salad
- Roasted Brussels Sprouts Salad
- Fennel and Orange Salad
- Smoked Salmon Salad

- Grilled Peach Salad
- Cucumber and Tomato Salad
- Creamy Avocado Salad
- Quinoa Tabbouleh Salad
- Mixed Green Salad with Nuts
- Balsamic Roasted Vegetable Salad
- Kale Caesar Salad
- Curried Chicken Salad
- Chickpea and Cucumber Salad
- Spicy Southwest Quinoa Salad
- Greek Yogurt Potato Salad

**Classic Caesar Salad**

**Ingredients:**

- romaine lettuce, chopped
- 1 cup croutons
- 1/2 cup grated Parmesan cheese
- 1/4 cup Caesar dressing
- Freshly cracked black pepper to taste

**Instructions:**

1. In a large bowl, toss romaine lettuce with Caesar dressing until coated.
2. Add croutons and Parmesan cheese, then toss gently.
3. Season with black pepper before serving.

# Mediterranean Quinoa Salad

**Ingredients:**

- 1 cup quinoa, cooked
- 1 cup cherry tomatoes, halved
- 1 cucumber, diced
- 1/2 red onion, diced
- 1/2 cup Kalamata olives, pitted and sliced
- 1/2 cup feta cheese, crumbled
- 2 tablespoons olive oil
- 1 tablespoon red wine vinegar
- Salt and pepper to taste

**Instructions:**

1. In a large bowl, combine cooked quinoa, tomatoes, cucumber, onion, olives, and feta.
2. In a small bowl, whisk together olive oil, vinegar, salt, and pepper.
3. Drizzle the dressing over the salad and toss gently before serving.

## Spinach and Strawberry Salad

**Ingredients:**

- 4 cups fresh spinach
- 1 cup strawberries, sliced
- 1/4 cup walnuts, toasted
- 1/4 cup feta cheese, crumbled
- 2 tablespoons balsamic vinaigrette

**Instructions:**

1. In a large bowl, combine spinach, strawberries, walnuts, and feta.
2. Drizzle with balsamic vinaigrette and toss gently before serving.

## Greek Salad with Feta

**Ingredients:**

- 2 cups romaine lettuce, chopped
- 1 cucumber, diced
- 1 cup cherry tomatoes, halved
- 1/2 red onion, thinly sliced
- 1/2 cup Kalamata olives, pitted
- 1/2 cup feta cheese, crumbled
- 2 tablespoons olive oil
- 1 tablespoon red wine vinegar
- Oregano, salt, and pepper to taste

**Instructions:**

1. In a large bowl, combine lettuce, cucumber, tomatoes, onion, olives, and feta.
2. In a small bowl, whisk together olive oil, vinegar, oregano, salt, and pepper.
3. Drizzle the dressing over the salad and toss before serving.

## Caprese Salad with Balsamic Glaze

**Ingredients:**

- 2 large tomatoes, sliced
- 8 oz fresh mozzarella, sliced
- Fresh basil leaves
- 2 tablespoons olive oil
- Balsamic glaze for drizzling
- Salt and pepper to taste

**Instructions:**

1. On a serving platter, alternate layers of tomato and mozzarella slices.
2. Tuck fresh basil leaves in between.
3. Drizzle with olive oil and balsamic glaze, then season with salt and pepper before serving.

## Cobb Salad with Avocado

**Ingredients:**

- 4 cups mixed greens
- 1 cup cooked chicken, diced
- 1/2 cup bacon, cooked and crumbled
- 1/2 cup cherry tomatoes, halved
- 1 avocado, diced
- 1/4 cup blue cheese, crumbled
- 2 tablespoons red wine vinaigrette

**Instructions:**

1. In a large bowl, layer mixed greens, chicken, bacon, tomatoes, avocado, and blue cheese.
2. Drizzle with vinaigrette and toss gently before serving.

## Roasted Beet and Goat Cheese Salad

### Ingredients:

- 2 cups mixed greens
- 2 medium beets, roasted and sliced
- 1/4 cup goat cheese, crumbled
- 1/4 cup walnuts, toasted
- 2 tablespoons balsamic vinaigrette

### Instructions:

1. In a large bowl, combine mixed greens, roasted beets, goat cheese, and walnuts.
2. Drizzle with balsamic vinaigrette and toss gently before serving.

## Asian Sesame Chicken Salad

**Ingredients:**

- 4 cups mixed greens
- 1 cup cooked chicken, sliced
- 1/2 cup shredded carrots
- 1/2 cup sliced bell peppers
- 1/4 cup sliced almonds
- 2 tablespoons sesame dressing

**Instructions:**

1. In a large bowl, combine mixed greens, chicken, carrots, bell peppers, and almonds.
2. Drizzle with sesame dressing and toss gently before serving.

Enjoy these fresh and vibrant salads!

**Chickpea and Avocado Salad**

**Ingredients:**

- 1 can (15 oz) chickpeas, rinsed and drained
- 1 avocado, diced
- 1 cucumber, diced
- 1/4 red onion, diced
- 1/4 cup fresh cilantro, chopped
- Juice of 1 lime
- Salt and pepper to taste

**Instructions:**

1. In a bowl, combine chickpeas, avocado, cucumber, red onion, and cilantro.
2. Drizzle with lime juice, season with salt and pepper, and toss gently before serving.

**Watermelon and Feta Salad**

**Ingredients:**

- 4 cups watermelon, cubed
- 1 cup feta cheese, crumbled
- 1/4 cup fresh mint, chopped
- 2 tablespoons olive oil
- Juice of 1 lime
- Salt and pepper to taste

**Instructions:**

1. In a large bowl, combine watermelon, feta, and mint.
2. Drizzle with olive oil and lime juice, season with salt and pepper, and toss gently before serving.

**Arugula and Pear Salad**

**Ingredients:**

- 4 cups arugula
- 1 ripe pear, thinly sliced
- 1/4 cup walnuts, toasted
- 1/4 cup goat cheese, crumbled
- 2 tablespoons balsamic vinaigrette

**Instructions:**

1. In a large bowl, combine arugula, pear slices, walnuts, and goat cheese.
2. Drizzle with balsamic vinaigrette and toss gently before serving.

**Southwest Black Bean Salad**

**Ingredients:**

- 1 can (15 oz) black beans, rinsed and drained
- 1 cup corn (fresh or frozen)
- 1 bell pepper, diced
- 1/4 red onion, diced
- 1/4 cup cilantro, chopped
- Juice of 1 lime
- 1 teaspoon cumin
- Salt and pepper to taste

**Instructions:**

1. In a bowl, combine black beans, corn, bell pepper, red onion, and cilantro.
2. Drizzle with lime juice, sprinkle with cumin, salt, and pepper, and toss gently before serving.

**Thai Mango Salad**

**Ingredients:**

- 2 ripe mangoes, julienned
- 1 red bell pepper, thinly sliced
- 1/4 cup red onion, thinly sliced
- 1/4 cup cilantro, chopped
- Juice of 2 limes
- 1 tablespoon fish sauce (or soy sauce for vegetarian)
- 1 tablespoon sesame oil

**Instructions:**

1. In a large bowl, combine mango, bell pepper, red onion, and cilantro.
2. In a small bowl, whisk together lime juice, fish sauce, and sesame oil.
3. Drizzle the dressing over the salad and toss gently before serving.

**Kale and Apple Salad**

**Ingredients:**

- 4 cups kale, stems removed and chopped
- 1 apple, thinly sliced
- 1/4 cup walnuts, toasted
- 1/4 cup feta cheese, crumbled
- 2 tablespoons apple cider vinaigrette

**Instructions:**

1. In a large bowl, combine kale, apple slices, walnuts, and feta.
2. Drizzle with apple cider vinaigrette and toss gently before serving.

## Panzanella (Bread Salad)

**Ingredients:**

- 4 cups day-old bread, cubed
- 2 cups ripe tomatoes, chopped
- 1 cucumber, diced
- 1/2 red onion, thinly sliced
- 1/4 cup fresh basil, chopped
- 3 tablespoons olive oil
- 1 tablespoon red wine vinegar
- Salt and pepper to taste

**Instructions:**

1. In a bowl, combine bread, tomatoes, cucumber, red onion, and basil.
2. In a small bowl, whisk together olive oil, vinegar, salt, and pepper.
3. Drizzle dressing over the salad and toss gently before serving.

**Farro and Roasted Vegetable Salad**

**Ingredients:**

- 1 cup farro, cooked
- 2 cups mixed roasted vegetables (e.g., zucchini, bell peppers, carrots)
- 1/4 cup feta cheese, crumbled
- 2 tablespoons olive oil
- 1 tablespoon lemon juice
- Salt and pepper to taste

**Instructions:**

1. In a bowl, combine cooked farro, roasted vegetables, and feta.
2. Drizzle with olive oil and lemon juice, season with salt and pepper, and toss gently before serving.

Enjoy these refreshing and vibrant salads!

**Zucchini Noodle Salad**

**Ingredients:**

- 3 medium zucchinis, spiralized
- 1 cup cherry tomatoes, halved
- 1/2 cup bell pepper, diced
- 1/4 cup red onion, thinly sliced
- 1/4 cup fresh basil, chopped
- 2 tablespoons olive oil
- 1 tablespoon lemon juice
- Salt and pepper to taste

**Instructions:**

1. In a large bowl, combine zucchini noodles, cherry tomatoes, bell pepper, red onion, and basil.
2. Drizzle with olive oil and lemon juice, season with salt and pepper, and toss gently before serving.

**Lentil Salad with Herbs**

**Ingredients:**

- 1 cup cooked lentils (green or brown)
- 1/4 cup parsley, chopped
- 1/4 cup cilantro, chopped
- 1/4 cup green onions, sliced
- 1/4 cup red bell pepper, diced
- 2 tablespoons olive oil
- 1 tablespoon red wine vinegar
- Salt and pepper to taste

**Instructions:**

1. In a bowl, combine cooked lentils, parsley, cilantro, green onions, and red bell pepper.
2. In a small bowl, whisk together olive oil, vinegar, salt, and pepper.
3. Drizzle the dressing over the salad and toss gently before serving.

**Grilled Vegetable Salad**

**Ingredients:**

- 2 cups mixed vegetables (zucchini, bell peppers, eggplant, etc.)
- 2 tablespoons olive oil
- Salt and pepper to taste
- 4 cups mixed greens
- 1/4 cup balsamic vinaigrette

**Instructions:**

1. Preheat the grill. Toss vegetables with olive oil, salt, and pepper.
2. Grill until tender and slightly charred, about 5-7 minutes.
3. In a large bowl, combine mixed greens and grilled vegetables. Drizzle with balsamic vinaigrette and toss gently before serving.

**Tuna Niçoise Salad**

**Ingredients:**

- 2 cups mixed greens
- 1 can (5 oz) tuna, drained
- 1/2 cup green beans, blanched
- 1/4 cup cherry tomatoes, halved
- 1/4 cup Kalamata olives
- 2 hard-boiled eggs, quartered
- 2 tablespoons olive oil
- 1 tablespoon red wine vinegar
- Salt and pepper to taste

**Instructions:**

1. In a large bowl, arrange mixed greens, tuna, green beans, cherry tomatoes, olives, and hard-boiled eggs.
2. Drizzle with olive oil and vinegar, season with salt and pepper, and serve.

**Cabbage and Carrot Slaw**

**Ingredients:**

- 2 cups green cabbage, shredded
- 1 cup carrots, shredded
- 1/4 cup mayonnaise
- 1 tablespoon apple cider vinegar
- 1 tablespoon honey
- Salt and pepper to taste

**Instructions:**

1. In a bowl, combine cabbage and carrots.
2. In a small bowl, whisk together mayonnaise, vinegar, honey, salt, and pepper.
3. Pour dressing over the cabbage mixture and toss well before serving.

**Shrimp and Avocado Salad**

**Ingredients:**

- 1 pound cooked shrimp, peeled and deveined
- 1 avocado, diced
- 1 cup cherry tomatoes, halved
- 1/4 cup red onion, diced
- 2 tablespoons lime juice
- 2 tablespoons cilantro, chopped
- Salt and pepper to taste

**Instructions:**

1. In a bowl, combine shrimp, avocado, cherry tomatoes, and red onion.
2. Drizzle with lime juice, add cilantro, and season with salt and pepper. Toss gently before serving.

**Berry Spinach Salad**

**Ingredients:**

- 4 cups spinach
- 1 cup mixed berries (strawberries, blueberries, raspberries)
- 1/4 cup feta cheese, crumbled
- 1/4 cup walnuts, toasted
- 2 tablespoons balsamic vinaigrette

**Instructions:**

1. In a large bowl, combine spinach, mixed berries, feta, and walnuts.
2. Drizzle with balsamic vinaigrette and toss gently before serving.

**Citrus and Pomegranate Salad**

**Ingredients:**

- 2 cups mixed greens
- 1 orange, segmented
- 1 grapefruit, segmented
- 1/2 cup pomegranate seeds
- 1/4 red onion, thinly sliced
- 2 tablespoons olive oil
- 1 tablespoon lemon juice
- Salt and pepper to taste

**Instructions:**

1. In a large bowl, combine mixed greens, orange segments, grapefruit segments, pomegranate seeds, and red onion.
2. Drizzle with olive oil and lemon juice, season with salt and pepper, and toss gently before serving.

Enjoy these fresh and vibrant salads!

**Thai Peanut Salad**

**Ingredients:**

- 4 cups mixed greens
- 1 cup shredded carrots
- 1 red bell pepper, sliced
- 1 cup cucumber, julienned
- 1/4 cup fresh cilantro, chopped
- 1/4 cup peanuts, chopped
- 1/4 cup Thai peanut dressing

**Instructions:**

1. In a large bowl, combine mixed greens, carrots, bell pepper, cucumber, and cilantro.
2. Drizzle with Thai peanut dressing and toss gently. Top with chopped peanuts before serving.

**Roasted Carrot and Quinoa Salad**

**Ingredients:**

- 2 cups carrots, sliced and roasted
- 1 cup cooked quinoa
- 1/4 cup feta cheese, crumbled
- 1/4 cup walnuts, toasted
- 2 tablespoons olive oil
- 1 tablespoon balsamic vinegar
- Salt and pepper to taste

**Instructions:**

1. Preheat the oven to 400°F (200°C) and roast carrots until tender, about 20 minutes.
2. In a bowl, combine roasted carrots, quinoa, feta, and walnuts.
3. Drizzle with olive oil and balsamic vinegar, season with salt and pepper, and toss gently before serving.

**Cobb Pasta Salad**

**Ingredients:**

- 8 oz pasta (e.g., rotini or fusilli), cooked and cooled
- 1 cup cooked chicken, diced
- 1/2 cup bacon, cooked and crumbled
- 1/2 cup cherry tomatoes, halved
- 1 avocado, diced
- 1/4 cup blue cheese, crumbled
- 2 tablespoons ranch dressing

**Instructions:**

1. In a large bowl, combine pasta, chicken, bacon, cherry tomatoes, avocado, and blue cheese.
2. Drizzle with ranch dressing and toss gently before serving.

**Apple and Walnut Salad**

**Ingredients:**

- 4 cups mixed greens
- 1 apple, thinly sliced
- 1/4 cup walnuts, toasted
- 1/4 cup feta cheese, crumbled
- 2 tablespoons apple cider vinaigrette

**Instructions:**

1. In a large bowl, combine mixed greens, apple slices, walnuts, and feta.
2. Drizzle with apple cider vinaigrette and toss gently before serving.

**BBQ Chicken Salad**

**Ingredients:**

- 4 cups mixed greens
- 1 cup cooked chicken, shredded
- 1/2 cup corn (fresh or canned)
- 1/2 cup black beans, rinsed and drained
- 1/4 cup BBQ sauce
- 1/4 cup ranch dressing

**Instructions:**

1. In a large bowl, combine mixed greens, chicken, corn, and black beans.
2. Drizzle with BBQ sauce and ranch dressing, then toss gently before serving.

**Caprese Pasta Salad**

**Ingredients:**

- 8 oz pasta (e.g., penne), cooked and cooled
- 1 cup cherry tomatoes, halved
- 8 oz fresh mozzarella, cubed
- 1/4 cup fresh basil, chopped
- 2 tablespoons olive oil
- 1 tablespoon balsamic vinegar
- Salt and pepper to taste

**Instructions:**

1. In a large bowl, combine pasta, cherry tomatoes, mozzarella, and basil.
2. Drizzle with olive oil and balsamic vinegar, season with salt and pepper, and toss gently before serving.

## Couscous and Chickpea Salad

**Ingredients:**

- 1 cup couscous, cooked
- 1 can (15 oz) chickpeas, rinsed and drained
- 1 cucumber, diced
- 1 red bell pepper, diced
- 1/4 cup parsley, chopped
- 2 tablespoons olive oil
- Juice of 1 lemon
- Salt and pepper to taste

**Instructions:**

1. In a large bowl, combine couscous, chickpeas, cucumber, bell pepper, and parsley.
2. Drizzle with olive oil and lemon juice, season with salt and pepper, and toss gently before serving.

**Taco Salad with Lime Dressing**

**Ingredients:**

- 4 cups mixed greens
- 1 cup cooked ground beef or turkey
- 1 cup cherry tomatoes, halved
- 1/2 cup black beans, rinsed and drained
- 1 avocado, diced
- 1/4 cup shredded cheese
- 2 tablespoons lime juice
- 2 tablespoons olive oil
- Salt and pepper to taste

**Instructions:**

1. In a large bowl, combine mixed greens, ground meat, cherry tomatoes, black beans, avocado, and cheese.
2. Drizzle with lime juice and olive oil, season with salt and pepper, and toss gently before serving.

Enjoy these delicious and colorful salads!

## Mediterranean Pasta Salad

**Ingredients:**

- 8 oz pasta (e.g., rotini or penne), cooked and cooled
- 1 cup cherry tomatoes, halved
- 1/2 cup Kalamata olives, pitted and sliced
- 1/2 cup feta cheese, crumbled
- 1/4 cup red onion, diced
- 1/4 cup fresh parsley, chopped
- 2 tablespoons olive oil
- 1 tablespoon red wine vinegar
- Salt and pepper to taste

**Instructions:**

1. In a large bowl, combine cooked pasta, cherry tomatoes, olives, feta, red onion, and parsley.
2. Drizzle with olive oil and vinegar, season with salt and pepper, and toss gently before serving.

**Radish and Cucumber Salad**

**Ingredients:**

- 1 cup radishes, thinly sliced
- 1 cup cucumber, thinly sliced
- 1/4 red onion, thinly sliced
- 2 tablespoons fresh dill, chopped
- 2 tablespoons olive oil
- 1 tablespoon white wine vinegar
- Salt and pepper to taste

**Instructions:**

1. In a bowl, combine radishes, cucumber, red onion, and dill.
2. In a small bowl, whisk together olive oil, vinegar, salt, and pepper.
3. Drizzle dressing over the salad and toss gently before serving.

## Beet and Citrus Salad

**Ingredients:**

- 2 cups cooked beets, sliced
- 1 orange, segmented
- 1 grapefruit, segmented
- 1/4 cup goat cheese, crumbled
- 1/4 cup walnuts, toasted
- 2 tablespoons balsamic vinaigrette

**Instructions:**

1. In a large bowl, arrange beets, orange segments, and grapefruit segments.
2. Sprinkle with goat cheese and walnuts.
3. Drizzle with balsamic vinaigrette and serve.

## Honey Mustard Chicken Salad

**Ingredients:**

- 4 cups mixed greens
- 1 cup cooked chicken, shredded
- 1/2 cup cherry tomatoes, halved
- 1/4 cup cucumber, diced
- 1/4 cup red onion, thinly sliced
- 2 tablespoons honey mustard dressing

**Instructions:**

1. In a large bowl, combine mixed greens, chicken, cherry tomatoes, cucumber, and red onion.
2. Drizzle with honey mustard dressing and toss gently before serving.

**Roasted Brussels Sprouts Salad**

**Ingredients:**

- 2 cups Brussels sprouts, halved and roasted
- 1/4 cup dried cranberries
- 1/4 cup pecans, toasted
- 1/4 cup feta cheese, crumbled
- 2 tablespoons olive oil
- 1 tablespoon apple cider vinegar
- Salt and pepper to taste

**Instructions:**

1. In a bowl, combine roasted Brussels sprouts, cranberries, pecans, and feta.
2. Drizzle with olive oil and vinegar, season with salt and pepper, and toss gently before serving.

**Fennel and Orange Salad**

**Ingredients:**

- 1 bulb fennel, thinly sliced
- 2 oranges, segmented
- 1/4 cup red onion, thinly sliced
- 2 tablespoons olive oil
- 1 tablespoon lemon juice
- Salt and pepper to taste

**Instructions:**

1. In a large bowl, combine fennel, orange segments, and red onion.
2. Drizzle with olive oil and lemon juice, season with salt and pepper, and toss gently before serving.

**Smoked Salmon Salad**

**Ingredients:**

- 4 cups mixed greens
- 4 oz smoked salmon, sliced
- 1/2 avocado, sliced
- 1/4 cup red onion, thinly sliced
- 2 tablespoons capers
- 2 tablespoons lemon vinaigrette

**Instructions:**

1. In a large bowl, arrange mixed greens, smoked salmon, avocado, red onion, and capers.
2. Drizzle with lemon vinaigrette and serve.

**Grilled Peach Salad**

**Ingredients:**

- 2 peaches, halved and grilled
- 4 cups arugula
- 1/4 cup goat cheese, crumbled
- 1/4 cup walnuts, toasted
- 2 tablespoons balsamic glaze

**Instructions:**

1. In a large bowl, combine arugula, grilled peaches, goat cheese, and walnuts.
2. Drizzle with balsamic glaze before serving.

Enjoy these fresh and flavorful salads!

## Cucumber and Tomato Salad

**Ingredients:**

- 2 cups cucumber, diced
- 2 cups cherry tomatoes, halved
- 1/4 red onion, thinly sliced
- 1/4 cup fresh basil, chopped
- 2 tablespoons olive oil
- 1 tablespoon red wine vinegar
- Salt and pepper to taste

**Instructions:**

1. In a large bowl, combine cucumber, cherry tomatoes, red onion, and basil.
2. Drizzle with olive oil and vinegar, season with salt and pepper, and toss gently before serving.

**Creamy Avocado Salad**

**Ingredients:**

- 2 ripe avocados, diced
- 1/2 cup Greek yogurt
- 1 tablespoon lemon juice
- 1/4 cup red onion, diced
- 1/4 cup cilantro, chopped
- Salt and pepper to taste

**Instructions:**

1. In a bowl, mash the avocados slightly.
2. Stir in Greek yogurt, lemon juice, red onion, cilantro, salt, and pepper.
3. Mix until combined and serve immediately.

**Quinoa Tabbouleh Salad**

**Ingredients:**

- 1 cup cooked quinoa
- 1 cup parsley, finely chopped
- 1/2 cup mint, finely chopped
- 1/2 cup cherry tomatoes, diced
- 1/4 cup green onion, sliced
- 2 tablespoons olive oil
- Juice of 1 lemon
- Salt and pepper to taste

**Instructions:**

1. In a large bowl, combine cooked quinoa, parsley, mint, cherry tomatoes, and green onion.
2. Drizzle with olive oil and lemon juice, season with salt and pepper, and toss gently before serving.

**Mixed Green Salad with Nuts**

**Ingredients:**

- 4 cups mixed greens
- 1/4 cup almonds, toasted
- 1/4 cup walnuts, toasted
- 1/4 cup feta cheese, crumbled
- 2 tablespoons balsamic vinaigrette

**Instructions:**

1. In a large bowl, combine mixed greens, almonds, walnuts, and feta.
2. Drizzle with balsamic vinaigrette and toss gently before serving.

**Kale Caesar Salad**

**Ingredients:**

- 4 cups kale, stems removed and chopped
- 1/2 cup Caesar dressing
- 1/4 cup Parmesan cheese, grated
- 1/4 cup croutons

**Instructions:**

1. In a large bowl, combine kale and Caesar dressing.
2. Toss until the kale is well coated.
3. Top with Parmesan cheese and croutons before serving.

**Curried Chicken Salad**

**Ingredients:**

- 2 cups cooked chicken, diced
- 1/4 cup mayonnaise
- 2 tablespoons curry powder
- 1/4 cup raisins
- 1/4 cup celery, diced
- Salt and pepper to taste

**Instructions:**

1. In a bowl, combine chicken, mayonnaise, curry powder, raisins, and celery.
2. Season with salt and pepper and mix well. Serve chilled.

## Chickpea and Cucumber Salad

**Ingredients:**

- 1 can (15 oz) chickpeas, rinsed and drained
- 1 cup cucumber, diced
- 1/2 cup red onion, diced
- 1/4 cup parsley, chopped
- 2 tablespoons olive oil
- Juice of 1 lemon
- Salt and pepper to taste

**Instructions:**

1. In a bowl, combine chickpeas, cucumber, red onion, and parsley.
2. Drizzle with olive oil and lemon juice, season with salt and pepper, and toss gently before serving.

Enjoy these fresh and delicious salads!

## Spicy Southwest Quinoa Salad

**Ingredients:**

- 1 cup cooked quinoa
- 1 can (15 oz) black beans, rinsed and drained
- 1 cup corn (fresh, frozen, or canned)
- 1 red bell pepper, diced
- 1/2 cup red onion, diced
- 1/4 cup cilantro, chopped
- 1 jalapeño, seeded and minced (optional)
- 2 tablespoons lime juice
- 2 tablespoons olive oil
- 1 teaspoon cumin
- Salt and pepper to taste

**Instructions:**

1. In a large bowl, combine cooked quinoa, black beans, corn, bell pepper, red onion, cilantro, and jalapeño (if using).
2. In a small bowl, whisk together lime juice, olive oil, cumin, salt, and pepper.
3. Pour the dressing over the salad and toss gently to combine. Serve chilled or at room temperature.

**Greek Yogurt Potato Salad**

**Ingredients:**

- 2 lbs baby potatoes, halved
- 1 cup plain Greek yogurt
- 2 tablespoons Dijon mustard
- 1 tablespoon apple cider vinegar
- 1/4 cup red onion, finely chopped
- 1/4 cup celery, diced
- 1/4 cup pickles, diced (optional)
- 2 tablespoons fresh dill, chopped (or 1 teaspoon dried)
- Salt and pepper to taste

**Instructions:**

1. Boil the baby potatoes in salted water until tender, about 10-15 minutes. Drain and let cool.
2. In a large bowl, mix together Greek yogurt, Dijon mustard, apple cider vinegar, red onion, celery, pickles (if using), dill, salt, and pepper.
3. Add the cooled potatoes to the dressing and gently toss to coat. Serve chilled.

Enjoy your salads!

www.ingramcontent.com/pod-product-compliance
Lightning Source LLC
LaVergne TN
LVHW081505060526
838201LV00056BA/2947